FIFE
PORTRAIT OF A COUNTY 1910-1950
FROM RARE PHOTOGRAPHS

FIFE
PORTRAIT OF A COUNTY 1910-1950
FROM RARE PHOTOGRAPHS

RAYMOND LAMONT-BROWN
AND
PETER ADAMSON

FOREWORD

BY

SIR KENNETH JAMES DOVER, Kt.,

Chancellor of the University of St Andrews

ALVIE PUBLICATIONS ST ANDREWS

DEDICATION

Peter Adamson dedicates this book to Joanne, Mark and Christopher.
Raymond Lamont-Brown dedicates this book to Gillian.

First published in 1982 by
Alvie Publications
52 Buchanan Gardens
St Andrews KY16 9LX

ISBN 0 9506200 4 1

Printed in Scotland by
Spectrum Printing Company
Burlington Street
Edinburgh

Contents

ACKNOWLEDGEMENTS

The authors would like to express their gratitude and thanks to the following for their help and encouragement in the production of this book: Miss Andrea Kerr of the Kirkcaldy Museum & Art Gallery; Miss Martha Hamilton, Headmistress of St Leonard's School, St Andrews; Mr Christopher Neale, Senior Librarian i/c of Reference and Information Services on behalf of the Director of Libraries, Museums and Art Galleries, Dunfermline; Mr Garth Sterne of the Anstruther Fisheries Museum; and, Mr Gordon Christie of St Andrews.

Further thanks are expressed individually to the undermentioned copyright holders for their kind help and permission to reproduce photographs from their collections:

Kirkcaldy Museum & Art Gallery, 4, 10, 11, 24, 27, 28, 31, 33, 48, 51, 53, 74, 92, 93, 94, 95, 99, 104, 115, 116, 121, 127, 128, 131, 149, 154, 156
Bill Flett 'Cowie Collection', 5, 8, 9, 13, 72, 77, 78, 88
St Andrews Preservation Trust, 6, 23, 32, 33, 47, 87, 112, 116
Dunfermline Central Library, 7, 14, 16, 17, 18, 37, 40, 42, 84, 91, 100, 103, 105, 106, 124, 125, 137, 147, 148, 52, 161, 163, 165, 166
Cupar Library, 12, 19, 35, 73, 132
G. Normand, Cupar, 15, 21, 22, 133
Gordon Christie, St Andrews, 20, 108, 109, 122, 153, 155
Mrs Hilda Kirkwood, St Andrews, 25, 80, 142, 143, 144
A.H. Wilson, Macduff Post Office, East Wemyss, 26, 52, 65, 75, 85, 86, 117, 158
D. Kilgour, Kirkcaldy, 29, 30, 166
Sir John Gilmour, Bt., Montrave, 2, 3, 66
Miss Edith May, Rosyth, 36, 38, 45, 46
Mrs T.A. Jardine, Lower Largo, 39, 90
J. Cameron, Strathmiglo, 44
S. Rankine, Tayport, 49, 50
Mrs Mary Stark, St Andrews, 80
J. Blyth, Newton of Falkland, 1, 41, 51, 68, 97, 98, 102, 110, 162
Mr & Mrs Gordon, Kilconquhar, 43
University Library, St Andrews, 34, 54, 164
St Leonard's School, St Andrews, 69, 70
Anstruther Fisheries Museum, 71, 76
David Thomson, 89
Mrs I. Davidson, Leslie, 101, 123, 159, 160
Mrs Michael Chrichton Stuart of Falkland, 135, 139, 140
Guardbridge Paper Mill, 158

A special tribute is added by the authors to the work and memory of George Cowie, the St Andrews photographer, whose skill has produced an unsurpassed record of local and social history in Fife. From George Cowie's collection, now owned by the University of St Andrews, the following have been selected in tribute: 55-64, 67, 79, 81-83, 107, 111, 113, 114, 118, 119, 129, 130, 134, 141, 146, 150, 151

St Andrews, Fife   Raymond Lamont-Brown
Scotland   Peter Adamson
June 1982

FOREWORD

By Sir Kenneth James Dover, M.A., D.LITT., F.R.S.E., F.B.A.,
Chancellor of the University of St Andrews.

FIFE is not a spectacular place. Most foreign visitors to Scotland, once they have 'done' Edinburgh, head for the jagged, soaring skylines of Wester Ross, going rapidly past the tongue of land that lies between the Firth of Tay and the Firth of Forth.

When I have the chance to catch such visitors and keep them here for a day or two, I have only to drive them around, without comment, and they are captivated by the clarity of view, the subtlety of colours and the unending variety of scenes in miniature which Fife displays. Yet, writing about Fife as an incomer who first set eyes on it twenty-seven years ago, I am aware, and embarrassed by the awareness, that through force of circumstances I feel at home only in one half of it. East Fife and West Fife (they might more appropriately have been called North Fife and South Fife) differ greatly in their economic resources and structure. The difference is reflected in the striking dissimilarity of their representation in Parliament for the last sixty years or more. And the early morning smells different. Ten years ago, when local government was being reorganised in Scotland, there was a threat to dismember Fife, uniting part with the north side of the Tay and part with the south side of the Forth. At that time I often heard the geographer's adage, 'Mountains divide, rivers unite'. I dare say this tends by and large to be true, but not always; it depends how big the rivers are and what they are used for. In the event the people of Fife successfully asserted their claim to be recognised as a Region on their own. The old County is the new Region—unofficially, or at best semi-officially, the 'Kingdom' of Fife, though indentification of a royal dynasty whose power was confined to the Region is not easy.

Looking at old photographs is a sophisticated form of 'human-watching'. They may or may not show everything that photographer and subject wished to be shown, but they always show something else as well, only to be seen by the observer who looks at them from the vantage-point of a later age. Each of the admirable photographs contained in this book excites historical curiosity and provokes questions about the lives, feelings and attitudes of the people portrayed.

Kenneth Dover

1. Little Willie Grant of Newton of Falkland plays his penny whistle for admiring relatives and long-suffering neighbours. Circa 1910.

INTRODUCING FIFE 1910-1950

In the immense advance of events which transformed the Scotland of Queen Victoria into what it is today, the fortunes of Fife were inextricably bound up. Following the great Liberal revival which marked the commencement of the century—they kept power 1905-1915, first under Sir Henry Campbell-Bannerman, then under Rt. Hon. H.H. Asquith—Fife had her part in returning Liberal members; caring radicals who were, it is important to remember, as different from the Liberals of today as chalk is to cheese. These old-time Liberals were the epitome of the basic moral and religious values of Fifers who were deeply involved as any Scots in the First World War, the Great Depression, the rise of insular pacifism which followed, and the Second World War. As much as any county, and more than many, Fife was affected by modifications of the constitution, by changes in the balance of political parties—from Liberal dominance to the various guises of Socialism—and by the important social changes of 1910-1950. All these events were coloured by the comings and goings of four monarchs.

At ten o'clock in the morning of May 6, 1910, H.R.H. Prince George of Wales, Duke of York, went to Buckingham Palace and stayed all day. At seven o'clock that evening he sent for his wife the former Princess May of Teck. Together they watched the last earthly moments of the sovereign who had been hailed 'the uncle of Europe'. At a quarter before midnight Edward VII died while oxygen was being administered. 'What a loss to the Nation & to us all. God help us. . . .' Princess May recorded. 'I have lost my best friend and the best of fathers', Prince George himself wrote in his Diary. 'I never had a *(cross)* word with him in my life. I am heartbroken and overwhelmed with grief, but God will help me in my great responsibilities. . . .'

The new King, who was proclaimed from Cupar Cross to Dunfermline High Street under the style of George V, at nine o'clock in the morning of May 10, 1910, felt very inadequate for the job. For he would not have become King at all had not his brother Prince Albert Victor, Duke of Clarence and Avondale, died in 1892.

The Fife newspapers of the day, like the *Fife Herald & Journal* and the *Coast Chronicle* recorded the old King's passing and the county's loyalties to the new monarch. George Frederick Ernest Albert, King of Great Britain, Ireland and the British Dominions beyond the seas, Emperor of India, had been born in 1865 and was crowned on June 22, 1911. At the end of the year George V visited India, being the first British emperor to do so. His reign was to dominate the large part of the scope of this book. There were official and unofficial Coronation junketings all over Fife, and at Cupar their celebrations included the opening of Duffus Park, which had been a bounty of John C. Duffus, jute merchant in his 'Bonvil House & Estate' gift.

Further, the Fife newspapers eulogised how Edward VII, by his pacific influence, had left Britain strong, secure and at peace. Yet, within three years of his death the kingdom was seared with industrial disputes whose events even fired the souls of Socialist Fifers to dreams of bloody civil war of Bolshevik intensity. All this was brought into focus locally by the ostentatious display of wealth and extravagance by the middle-class and 'county' families in the face of unmitigated poverty and dissatisfaction. Between 1909 and 1913 industrial disputes doubled to 1800 as recorded by the Labour Dept. of the Board of Trade.

Within two more years, the new King's whole Empire was embroiled in the costliest conflict it had ever known. The outbreak of the war against Germany in August 1914 was a consequence of the German desire for world power and her lack of sea ports and colonies. The excuse for hostilities came with the murder of the Austro-Hungarian Archduke Franz Ferdinand and his wife at Sarajevo, Yugoslavia, on June 28, 1914. When Germany invaded neutral Belgium the British were forced to declare war. From all over Fife men were mustered to the colours. Cupar, for instance, was the headquarters of the Lowland Mounted Brigade, and the Queen's Own Glasgow Yeomanry trained in East Fife.

The Fifers who went to war left behind them a county that had changed vastly in the forerunning hundred years. The dichotomy of rich and poor was slowly diminishing in real terms. The spread of popular education, the growth of trade unionism and the increased mobility of fellow Fifers were to lead to many more fundamental changes for those who were lucky enough not to be blown to pieces in the Flanders mud.

Over the years following the Armistice on November 11, 1918, war memorials proliferated from Freuchie to Springfield, and from Ladybank to Anstruther. Earl Douglas Haig, whose war of attrition has been adversely criticised for the terrible loss of life it involved, personally honoured the dead by unveiling the war memorial at St Andrews on September 23, 1922.

The end of the First World War brought a lifting of the darkness of apprehension and an abatement to the spiritual numbness of the preceding four years. They had been the worst years that Fifers had ever known. Years of dreading to answer the door for fear of being handed a War Office telegram bringing news of the death of a son, brother, or husband. Years of hesitating to open the *Scotsman*, or the *Courier* with their long casualty lists. Those horrendous years consumed much of Fife's youth and too many of the older men needed to put the economy right with the coming of peace. Yet, now it was all over, the immediate terror, grief and worry vanished with the discomforts and inconveniences. Khaki and navy blue uniforms disappeared from the cafés and thoroughfares, and butter and sugar appeared again on the shelves. And those whose eyes still misted at the first strains of the soldiers' plaintive song 'There's a Long, Long, Trail . . .' now buckled down to make a new life, and regain the hope of the sunny summer of 1914.

Soldiers returning to Fife towns and villages found many changes, not least in their domestic lives. Their infants had grown into unrecognisable children; their wives had had a taste of working life in the factories of Kirkcaldy and Dunfermline and on the farms of East Fife. So it was as difficult for the wives as for their demobbed husbands to settle back into workaday routines with comparative strangers, depressed and shellshocked. Consumer goods like clothes and furniture were scarce; rationing restricted food supplies to 'fair shares for all' at least in the towns, but in the country districts farm produce became the new currency. Food prices were to remain fairly high until the Spring of 1921: Eggs then became around 2s. 8d (13½p) per doz; Bacon, 2s. 4d (11½p) per lb; Butter, 2s. 10d (14p) per lb; and, Rice 6d (2½p) per lb. (NB: *All the decimal prices in this book should be multiplied by eight to arrive at a rough comparative figure for today*).

From 1910 to 1921 (the year of the first post-war census) trends of population in Fife changed. In 1921, there were 1096 females for every 1000 males. The war was partly to blame—the increased numbers of 'unclaimed treasures', as spinsters were called, in the teashops of St Andrews and Dunfermline, showed the imbalance—but the main reason was the higher death rate in infancy of boy babies. More Fifers now lived to be 65 and there were fewer children under 15.

Liberal Coalition Prime Minister Lloyd George's electioneering promise to build 'a fit country for heroes to live in' soon went sour, for the returning heroes readily saw how the

10

2. Edward, probably the most popular Prince of Wales in history. His reign as Edward VIII ended in abdication because of his determination to marry the American divorcee Mrs Wallis Simpson.

3. Sir John Gilmour in Court Dress, with Their Majesties, King George V and Queen Mary.

inequalities of society with its strong class divisions had survived. Over 75 per cent of people in Fife in 1921 owned goods and savings amounting to no more than £100. Fife's middle class now ranging from the ex-country gentleman (who were increasingly hit by higher taxes and death duties), doctors, clergymen and civil servants to shopkeepers and clerks, tended to live reasonable well. They bought the new cars, drank the new cocktails and sent their children to feepaying schools. Yet, as the 1920s developed life for the Fife working class, the mining, factory and agricultural workers, changed more radically than the upper and middle income groups. As their savings dwindled the middle class became more nervous of the workers but found a champion in Stanley Baldwin, the Conservative Party Prime Minister who governed Britain almost continuously from 1923 until he retired in 1937. Baldwin, described by fellow-Tory Lord Curzon as 'a man of the utmost insignificance' belied his unsmart exterior. He was a shrewd politician who managed to restore stable government.

Politically Fife remained radical during the years 1910-1950. By 1910 the county was overwhelmingly Liberal, and was represented by five MPs. One new boy appeared in 1910, James Duncan Millar who was elected to represent St Andrews Burghs for the Liberals. West Fife was represented by John Deans Hope, the National Liberal; he had won the seat in 1910, but it fell to the ex-miner William Adamson of Wemyss for Labour in Dec 1910 (in 1906 the Liberals had broken their alliance with Labour, deciding to oppose all Socialist candidates). East Fife had been represented by the Rt. Hon. H. H. Asquith (Liberal Prime Minister, 1908, Coalition Prime Minister, 1915), a Gladstonian Liberal since 1886, and Kirkcaldy Burghs was held for the Liberals by Sir James Henry Dalziel until 1921. In those days, Dunfermline, Inverkeithing, Culross and South Queensferry were in the Stirling Burghs constituency, which had been held by Arthur Ponsonby, son of Sir Henry Ponsonby, Queen Victoria's private secretary, since 1908.

The Representation of the People Act of 1918 introduced great changes. Four constituencies were now evolved for the county: East Fife; West Fife; Kirkcaldy Burghs and Dunfermline Burghs. All Fife males over 21 could now vote. A woman had to be 30 before she could vote and even then she could only do so if she or her husband owned property worth £5 per year. Votes for women over 21 came from the Conservative government of Stanley Baldwin in 1928. By that time St Andrews University shared with Edinburgh University in returning one member (Rt. Hon. Sir Robert Findlay, Unionist, 1910)—the university seats were abolished in the Representation of the People Act, 1948. Those were the days of great local interest in party manifestoes and general political fervour, and election campaigns tended to be hectic and abusive. By 1950 the pendulum had swung Labour's way. W. W. Hamilton represented West Fife (he had defeated the Communist MP, Willie Gallacher, who had been returned in 1935); T. F. Hubbard was Labour's man in Kirkcaldy and J. Clunie represented the Socialists in Dunfermline. Only East Fife remained right wing radical, returning J. Henderson Stewart for the National Liberal & Conservatives. One local man did achieve high office. The Rt. Hon. Sir John Gilmour Bt., (1876-1940) of Lundin and Montrave, became Secretary of State for Home Affairs in 1932 in J. Ramsay Macdonald's Coalition government.

In 1910 Fife was still organised in terms of local government by the 1889 Act. In 1890 the Fife County Council had been set up with the Earl of Elgin and Kincardine as its first chairman. The Local Government Scotland Act of 1929 abolished parish councils and transferred to County Councils the major functions of the small burghs. In some ways this was prejudicial to old traditions and local patriotism in Fife. The Act broke up all the old School Boards with their religious and sectarian cranks and patronising 'do-gooders', and established the system by which members were chosen both on general grounds of expertise and the more insidious lines of party politics. In 1892 there had been 139 schools in Fife, by 1948 there were 164.

In 1918, of course, a Fife child's education depended upon the status of his family. The upper classes in Fife invariably sent their children to expensive boarding schools at 13, then to public school. The middle class child usually went to High Schools at 11, and stayed until 16 or 18. Intelligent working class children could proceed from the Fife burgh schools to the High Schools by way of a scholarship. At the end of the First World War, forty percent of Fife children left school before 14. Previous to that war it was not unusual in Fife for children to work on farms for three days a week. The Labour Government of 1924 proposed the '11+' examination for streaming children into secondary education.

Learning by rote was continued throughout this period as the best way of absorbing information for public examinations. The formal teaching methods of pre-1918, however, were relaxed as lessons became more interesting and teachers were less obsessed with the problems of discipline. This period was a time, too, when adults wanted to educate themselves as well as their children. So groups from the Workers' Education Association to the Womens' Rural Institute stepped up their adult education facilities.

The National Health Insurance Act of 1911 was to cause many changes in health care in Fife. The Act was designed to assure the breadwinner against loss of income as a result of illness, death, or unemployment. The benefits were not felt until January 1913 when the Act became operative; now the county's doctors were paid 9s (45p) capitation fee per patient. Prescriptions had to be paid for in full at chemists' shops, or at the doctor's dispensary. The Act set up school medical services for the early detection and prevention of disease in children. Fife children now became used to regular inspections for head lice and routine

4. Mrs. J.H. Thomas and Mrs Stanley Baldwin in animated conversation while their husbands stand in stoic silence. L. to R.: Sir John Gilmour, Secretary for Scotland; former Labour Colonial Secretary James Henry Thomas, who left public life in disgrace over revealing budget secrets; future Prime Minister Neville Chamberlain; and, Conservative Prime Minister Stanley Baldwin.

hygiene tests. Diseases from indifferent diet (ie, rickets) were common and some 80 percent of all Fife school children had advanced dental caries (there were no school dentists employed by the County). There was no such thing, either, as School Dinners; sometimes a philanthropist like the lino tycoon Sir Michael Nairn (1874-1952) of Kirkcaldy would fund the setting up of a Soup Kitchen (a 'Soupie') for the feeding of poor children. Working class children suffered too, from foot infections as many had no footwear and the clothes they owned were worn summer and winter. Bootless Bairns Funds, like the one set up in Kirkcaldy in the early 1920s supported by charity did supply heavy tacketed boots for some children.

Fife general practitioners still had a large amount of private practice (some doctors had separate doors to their surgeries for private patients). Right into the 1920s many working class patients felt that it was wise to seek private consultations if they had anything more than a common ailment. They believed that they would receive better treatment if they paid for it. Many of the smaller hospitals in Fife relied on private finance for their establishment and to endow beds (a case in point was the Wemyss Memorial Hospital, 1909). The 1930s saw a therapeutic revolution, yet it was not until the National Health Act of 1946 that every Fife family received nationally funded health care.

The fashionable woman in Fife in 1910 was encircled by kilometers of feather boa and was overshadowed by vast hats trimmed with ribbons and feathers, or the whole stuffed with birds and fruit. She wore little, lace-covered boleros and rose like a nymph, corseted in whalebone instruments of torture, from her sweeping circular skirt, her bodice glittering with beads. Parasols, or umbrellas, were carried by anyone wishing to be considered well turned out. The Fife male was dressed mostly in black, as if in perpetual mourning. Only in capes and overcoats was there any hint of colour or imagination. The photographs in this book show that most professional men in Fife during 1900-1918 invariably wore frock-coat, or jacket, over dark trousers, a tie secured with a tiepin, a top hat and gloves. Underclothes tended towards the mummification of both sexes in 1910 and did not really change amongst the folk of Fife up to the Second World War. Fashion mostly originated in France, with the elegant Fifer shopping in London, Edinburgh and Dundee, while lesser folk began to flock to the developing department stores. After the Second World War fashion trends switched from France to Italy, but the working class Fifer throughout the period 1910 to 1950 tended to be somewhat ten years behind fashion and still favoured the darker colours and thicker materials as 'serviceable' and economic.

Sport, bicycling and motoring all had their effects on fashion and by the First World War children's clothes were being tailored specially for them and veered away from making them 'miniature adults'. The end of the war brought a yearning for bright colours and women expressed their new independence by bobbing their hair, smoking Craven A and sporting trousers. The Fife female of the 1920s indulged regularly in hairdressing, cosmetics, shorter skirts and perfume. Even up to the late 1940s the Fife male was not really dynamic in terms of fashion, and had few aberrations of taste like the ultra-wide trousers known as 'Oxford bags', which had been adopted by all smart young men of 1924.

Reliance on the old industries—Fife could contribute coal, engineering, papermaking, fish curing, distillery, milling, shipping and agriculture—had been too great before the First World War, and in the 1920s the economic picture was disasterous. As the decades between the wars evolved, there was a drop of 20 percent in those employed in agriculture in Fife. The prosperity of 1914-18 was short lived, mechanisation axed jobs and markets for Fife farm products declined in the face of overseas competition. Fife farmers did embrace new ideas and remained in the forefront of farming counties, but farmers were now loaded with loan debts. One great change which occurred during the period of this book, was the gradual phasing out of teams of horses. Fife was known for its horse-mills, those conical, octagonal additions to farm buildings in which horses plodded round and round a vertical shaft providing energy to link to driving gear. Steam tractors and steam traction engines of Victoria's day were steadily replaced by petrol-driven tractors. Farms in Fife were run on a cash-crop basis, with cattle and sheep an essential concomitant, yet they had become smaller in acreage. In 1947 Fife had 2179 agricultural holdings compared with 1109 in 1867; even so with an average of 103.6 acres the farms of Fife were larger than elsewhere in Scotland.

When the government declared that they could not guarantee the minimum price of corn, pay packets had to be cut. In the 1920s farm labourers received 28s (£1.40) for a 50 hour week instead of the 42s (£2.10) for the 48 hour week they had worked in 1917. By 1947 the minimum weekly wage in agriculture was 90s (£4.50) for men and 75s. 6d (£3.77) for women.

Many Fife workers out of work at this time went 'on the Dole' as the 1920 Unemployment Benefit System was called—this was often referred to as the 'burroo', a Scotticism for 'Bureau'. Men received 15s (75p) per week and women 12s (60p); but, this benefit could only be claimed for 15 weeks of the year. Extra money was paid through Fife's Poor Law Guardians, but the county now saw the horrors of a new poverty. Parish Relief worked out at 7s. 6d (37½p) per adult and 1s (5p) per week for children under 14. These became the days of the snack trade in which people ate cheaply; in Fife cafés, a 3-course lunch could be obtained for 1s. 6d (7½p).

Initially the pits took up much of the surplus workers who had been laid off in agriculture in Fife. The Fife Coal Company (Est. 1872) was one of the biggest employers and expanded to take in the Earl of Rosslyn's Collieries Ltd and the Oakley Collieries in 1923 and 1924 respectively. At the outbreak of the First World War, Fife was producing 9 million tons of coal, of which 5 million tons were for export.

It was with the miners that the labour struggles were to receive their initial driving force. When the private owners received their mines back in 1921, they terminated all existing contracts with their employees and introduced lower wages. The miners had been discontented with their lot since the Armistice and in accord with the rest of the country the Fife branch of the Miners' Federation voted in 1921 for a strike. At this stage the miners were forced to accept reduced pay packets, but when a Royal Commission once again recommended cuts in the miners' wages the General Strike began on May 4, 1926. As a consequence the gates of the Fife Coal Co—from Cowdenbeath and Blairadam Collieries to the Donibristle and Bowhill Collieries— were locked.

The General Strike collapsed in twelve days, but the Coal Strike continued. Slowly, forced by hunger to accept longer hours and less pay, the miners returned to work. To earn a few coppers the miners who did not find work busked through the streets and villages of Fife, receiving plates of kail and stovies by way of further payment. On Nov 25, 1926, the Fife mines reopened and Sir Charles Carlow Reid declared that the strike had cost the Fife Coal Company alone £133,000—no-one had won and the stage was set for more penury.

Fife's fishing industry could offer no succour for the increasing unemployed. Around 1910 the motor boat began to appear in large numbers in Fife harbours; although the steam drifter was popular until the 1920 decline. Trade in Fife was greatly affected by the mysterious movements of the herring. During 1910-1914 there were good earnings to be had and new boats were bought; the First World War brought an artificially prosperous time which heightened the depressed trends of the industry in the early 1920s. From the late 1920s to the 1930s catches were consistently high and stable. The Second World War drained to the services both boats and men. Herrings now deserted the Forth, so that by 1950 there were none.

The depression in all facets of industry which hit Britain began with the Wall Street crash of October 1929. As the dollar collapsed European countries could no longer pay their war debts or finance reconstruction with American loans. Britain suffered as European countries withdrew their gold from the Bank of England. Ramsay Macdonald's second Labour government of June 8, 1929, had to face an over-valued pound, the trade recession and world depression. No-one wanted the products from Fife and unemployment soared to a new national peak of 2,849,025 in 1932. To ration the demand for benefits the National Government led by Labourite Ramsay Macdonald as Prime Minister introduced the emotive Means Test. The workingman's dole became subject to a scale relating to household needs. Now officials visited Fife homes, checking up on the savings and expenditure of husband and wife: Thus a child could not earn a few pennies on a newspaper round, or a working girl accept a shilling rise without it being deducted from the family dole. Benefits in 1934 began to be administered nationally by the Unemployment Assistance Board. A BBC roving reporter quoted in 1934 the case of a Fife labourer who had had one year's work in 12 and whose family of five lived on 33s (£1.65) per week; their diet being bread, margarine and tea. Only rearmament was to bring down the unemployment figures and increase wages.

On January 20, 1936, Fife was plunged into mourning for a beloved King who died, aged seventy, at Sandringham in the presence of Queen Mary and his children. Pictures of George V appeared, draped with black crêpe in shop windows all over the county. Folk in Fife had caught a glimpse of George V when he and Queen Mary stayed at Broomhall, as a guest of the Earl of Elgin and his Countess, daughter of Lord Cochrane of Cults.

15

On May 6, 1935, George V had been given the unprecedented honour of a Jubilee to celebrate the twenty-fifth anniversary of his accession. Fife folk played a part in this personal tribute to a King they recognised as a constitutional sovereign and both Labour and Unionist alike wore red, white and blue favours and joined the soirées. In Kirkcaldy the Communists daubed slogans of an anti-monarchist nature on walls and pavements, their loyalties being not to 'King and Country' but to the government of Soviet Russia. George V, in 1932, started his Sovereign's Christmas Message to nation and commonwealth, via BBC microphones. His gruff tones, warmly resonant and paternal, had endeared him to his Fife subjects who now sincerely and genuinely grieved his passing. There were many in Fife who shared George V's misgivings about the qualities of his son, the new King.

Edward VIII was an unmarried, forty-one year old King who looked and behaved as though he was ten years younger. As Prince of Wales his unconventional approach to his public duties and his good looks had made him a real 'Prince Charming'. Edward became Captain of the Royal and Ancient Golf Club and visited St Andrews to 'play himself in' on Sept 27, 1922. Again in 1933 he made an official visit to the unemployment centres of Leven, Cupar and St Andrews, staying with the Earl of Elgin at Broomhall. For his visit to Newport and Dundee, Edward stayed at Rusack's Marine Hotel, St Andrews, and made a special visit to the Argyle Brewery.

The character faults of the new King—his irresponsible behaviour over public duties, his shifting personality, his immature outlook—cancelled out in the minds of many his immense popularity when Prince of Wales. Less than eleven months after his succession he left England as the Duke of Windsor bent on marriage to twice divorced Mrs Ernest Simpson. His abdication was an unprecedented act which split Fife society. Many Fifers saw his failure to observe the sacred trust of his birth as a betrayal. His activities were avidly followed in the Fife papers: In December 1936, Edward left for France to a self-imposed exile that lasted 35 years; he died in 1972.

Britain now had a new Royal Family. The shy, stuttering George VI—born H.R.H. Prince Albert Frederick Arthur George ('Bertie' to his family), Duke of York—was to prove a very popular monarch despite not being 'born for the job'. In this he was devotedly supported by his much-admired wife, the former Lady Elizabeth Bowes Lyon, daughter of the Earl and Countess of Strathmore, who was to forge close links with Fife social and academic as pictures in this collection show.

Soccer, Tennis, Curling, Bowls, Golf, Dancing, Concerts, the Cinema were the main sports and away-from-home entertainments of the period in Fife. Associations like the Womens' Rural Institute and the various church guilds flourished too. Beginning after the First World War church attendance began to decline in Fife as a more secular spirit entered society. Not only had scientific discoveries shaken beliefs in the literal assessment of the gospels, but young people actively fought against the rituals of church-going. In 1900 the Free Church (1100 parishes) had joined the United Presbyterians (600 congregations) to form the United Free Church. In 1929 the U.F. united with the Auld Kirk and the modern Kirk of Scotland resulted. Through 1910 to 1950 the Episcopal Church retained its independent position, Fife being in the diocese of St Andrews, Dunkeld and Dunblane. By and large the Roman Catholic congregations in Fife were small, but the county did rank an Archbishop (of St Andrews and Edinburgh); these congregations swelled as ex-patriot Poles established communities, like that in St Andrews, following the Second World War.

Apart from the newspapers circulating in Fife there was a great demand for popular fiction. Edgar Wallace, Nat Gould, Dorothy Sayers and Agatha Christie were amongst those who supplied the escapism which led to a boom in the 'twopenny libraries'. By the 1930s, small stationers and tobacconists rented books from wholesale libraries charging 2d (1p) loan per book; Boots the Chemists had over a million books in their lending libraries. Many folk were introduced to books through unemployment. Among the popular Scottish authors who had Fife connections were Andrew Lang (1844-1912, first Gifford Lecturer in Natural Theology at St Andrews University), Sir James Matthew Barrie (1860-1937, Rector of St Andrews) and John Buchan (1875-1940, whose father had been minister of Pathhead Free Church, Kirkcaldy).

Radio, or 'the wireless' as it was called, arrived in 1922 and quickly achieved prominence as a news medium. In 1926 the British Broadcasting Company was transformed into the British Broadcasting Corporation. The BBC was to know Scottish influence early as Sir John Reith (later Lord Reith) insisted on the importance of 'the high moral tone' of his Calvinist background in broadcasting. In the early days listening to the radio was not a simple pleasure. You needed crystal sets, 'cats' whiskers', ear-phones, and aerials. In the 1930s the radio became a piece of furniture incorporating loudspeakers. By 1939 three families in four in Fife owned a radio, but in the 1940s the development of television (transmissions started in 1936) was to become the main home entertainment boosted by the Succession in 1952 and the Coronation of Elizabeth II on the death of George VI.

One form of transport which greatly developed in Fife after the First World War was the 'bus. Many of Fife's early 'buses were lorries fitted with special bodies for Saturday afternoon work. There were a great many 'bus concerns in Fife from 1910 to the 1920s, but by 1936 W. Alexander & Sons had become a conglomerate and a wide network of services evolved in the county. Leisure travel in Fife was provided for the masses by the introduction of opulent coaches in the 1930s, but the expense of such 'buses (and the advent of the Second World War) meant that the 1933 Leyland Tiger TS6s and the 1938 AEC Regal 10T10s of the Fife county services were still in harness until the 1950s. The 1920s were boom years for motor sales, a 9/20 HP Rover could be purchased for £185 in 1926 and by 1927 one family in 12 in Fife owned a car. Country folk continued to hate cars and motor cycles and petitioned Queen Mary 'to help us get some relief from the motor cars'—the Queen was unable to help!

As the 1930s developed the spectre of war began to creep again into the minds of Fifers. The rise of National Socialism in Germany and that country's re-armament encouraged social nervousness. In 1933 Adolf Hitler was appointed Chancellor by Hindenburg and Germany was set on a collision course with both Soviet Russia and the Western Allies. The British navy was mobilised in 1938 when Austria was annexed by Germany and warships were seen once again in the Forth and off the East Neuk. On September 3rd, 1939, war was declared between Britain and Germany, and Fife was again put on a war footing as concrete and brick defences, observer stations and emergency airstrips were developed. Deprivation lasted until the victory over Japan on Sept 2nd, 1945, celebrated the end of the Second World War. Some of the pictures herein speak poignantly of the dispossessions and restrictions, and of the personalities, of the two World Wars and how they related to Fife.

The years 1910 to 1950 marked the real development of the snapshot photograph, following the introduction of the 'Brownie' camera in February 1900 by the Eastman Kodak Co of Rochester, New York. It was advertised in Fife papers to 'make pictures 2¼ x 2¼ inches'. 'Load in daylight', the adverts read, 'with our six exposure film cartridges, (they) are so simple that they can be easily operated by a School Boy or Girl'. By 1903, 50,000 of these cameras had been sold in Britain making it possible to dispense with the very expensive and cumbersome photographic equipment of the Victorian photographer.

When war broke out in 1914, there was a boom in photographic business in Fife, reaching a peak in 1917. People bought cameras to photograph loved ones leaving for France, and soldiers bought them to take abroad; it was, of course, a court martial offence to take photographs while on active service. Because of this the small 'Vest Pocket Kodak' camera (easily concealable) was popular.

Following the First World War, there was an increase in photographic sales. New materials were now used in camera production. The popular Bakelite APeM camera of 1928 (the Rajar No 6) was sold through Fife newsagents and confectioners. Many Fifers saved up gift coupons from Black Cat cigarettes, Cadbury's chocolates, or Wright's Coal Tar Soap to obtain their first camera. Despite the Depression there was a high increase in the popularity of photography in the 1930s. The bulk of photographic equipment sales (and developing) was still very much the preserve of the local chemists' shops; the camera shop we know today was a post-1950 phenomenon. Cameras (15s to 21s—75p to £1.05) and films (1s, or 5p, each) became cheaper and the plastic moulded variety of camera boomed from the mid 1930s. When the Second World War broke out, photography was an essential part of family life. The 5s (25p) camera of 1939 was well within the reach of virtually every home. The needs of war led to new techniques in photography and these were passed on to the consumer in the late 1940s following the ending of post-war emergency economic measures.

Throughout 1910-1950 many Fife photographers made news for themselves. Frank Findlay, for instance, was a wellknown Auchtermuchty photographer around 1910, and his work was popular in the *Fife News Almanac*, as was that of W. Patrick of St Andrews. Perhaps the most popular and most celebrated Fife commercial and press photographer was George Cowie of St Andrews. He began his photographic business (at 131 South Street) in St Andrews in 1931 and was taking photographs for the UK press up to his death in 1982. During the years covered by this book the professional photographers used the glass plate Speed Graphic, VN, and Sanderson-¼ Plate cameras.

This collection is an anthology taken from the best extant snapshot and professional photographs of the period. Indeed the photographs, often deliberately unposed (and with little thought to formal composition) are a rich source of interest for the social historian, the connoisseur of costume and the student of many now vanished ways of life.

St Andrews, 1982   RAYMOND LAMONT-BROWN

DOWN TO THE SEA IN SHIPS

ALTHOUGH the Scottish shipbuilding industry was to be severely hit by the loss of overseas markets after 1918, the contraction was not harshly felt along the Fife shore. The Forth continued to be known for its breaking and repair yards at Rosyth and Inverkeithing, and the era of rapid technological change did not affect the small wooden boat industry. For instance, J. N. Miller & Sons Ltd of St Monace weathered the financial storms and the Burntisland Shipping Co Ltd, established in 1918, became known for their small tramp steamers and coastal colliers. So, Fife-built ships went to Argentina, Egypt, Norway and Portugal, and pay packets were swollen by the lucrative scrapping of the German High Seas Fleet of warships scuttled in Scapa Flow. Fife folk witnessed the comings and goings of the great British warships in an age when the diplomacy of nations was governed by the capital ship and its firepower. As Admiral of the Fleet Lord Chatfield said: 'The British battleship is like the queen on the chessboard . . . Properly supported by other weapons, it is the final arbiter at sea; to lose it is to lose the game'.

The 1920s and 1930s were the heydays of the cruise liners, and the Forth saw many a liner. For just over £20 the well-to-do could sail from the Fife coast on a fortnight's cruising to the Norwegian fiords.

4. The stately liner *Leviathan*, built for the Hamburg-America Line in May 1914, steams up the Forth. Of 48,943 tons, the liner was sold for scrap in 1938, and here dwarfs the Firth of Forth ferry and pilot boats.

5. GW4 *Teresa Watterston* ran aground off Anstruther to the consternation of local fishermen and the delight of small boys in the mid-1930s.

6. The *Princess Wilhelmina* of Halmnstad, Sweden, languishes on the West Sands, St Andrews, September 29th, 1912. Nine of her crew were rescued by the St Andrews lifeboat *The John and Sarah Hatfield*, under Coxswain Chisholm.

7. Launched on February 4th, the King Edward VII Class battlecruiser *Zealandia* enters No 1 dock Rosyth (the first ship ever to do so) on March 27th, 1916. She saw action in the Dardanelles, November 1915, and was sold November 8th, 1921.

8. A few of the St Monance fishing fleet await high tide. On the hill sits foursquare the distinctive church, a landmark for the Forth fishermen.

(Overleaf)
9. The Anstruther fleet cluster around the lighthouse, getting steam up for their next trip.

10. Methil Dock—the new one opened January 1913—seen here through the archway with its Coal Drop, was an important coal shipping quay. As early as 1795 a horse-operated railroad had brought coal to Methil from the collieries of the Earl of Wemyss.

11.   Horse-waggons being loaded at Kirkcaldy harbour with corking for the Michael Nairn & Co linoleum factory (seen to the left of the photograph, background), circa 1930.

12.   A paddle steamer—popular on day trips on the Forth—noses in to Largo Pier, circa 1910. Once the St Andrews stage coaches linked with the Largo Pier/Newhaven Ferry.

13. Anstruther Lifeboat makes a proud display on Gala Day, circa 1950. Until the 1940s Anstruther was the capital of herring fishing in Scotland during the winter months.

14. A sailing boat stands off Culross Pier, circa 1910. In the 17th century this was a flourishing sea port for the cruive fishing trade and the nearby coal mines and salt pans.

WORLD WAR I : 1914-1918

'THE victory of Germany will be a victory of soul over numbers. The German soul is opposed to the pacifist ideal of civilisation, for is not peace an element of evil corruption?' Thus wrote the liberal humanist Thomas Mann (1875-1955) of the philosophy that was sweeping through Kaiser William II's Germany. A philosophy which sank Europe into a war which was to topple thrones and alter a way of life for millions that had been forged over centuries.

From the outbreak of hostilities, August 4th 1914, the General Staff of the British Army and Navy were fully aware of the vulnerability of the coast of Fife, and the 'plum targets' for the Germans of the Forth Bridge and the Rosyth Dockyard. The Forth and the Fife coast became the defensive position to be protected by the 3rd (Special Reserve) Battalion of the Black Watch under Major R.E. Anstruther, MC. Should the Germans pierce the Fife defences, they were to be harrassed from over the Tay by a division of the 3rd Seaforths known as the 'Cromarty Brigade'. In reality Fife held fast and sent many of her sons abroad, some to serve in such units as the Fife and Forfar Yeomanry, which on New Year's Day 1917 became the 14th Battalion, The Black Watch. Letters came home to Fife from all the theatres of war from Egypt to Gallipoli and from France to the Dardanelles.

15. Black Watch Colour-Sergeant Ripley, V.C., waits at his post in Crossgates, Cupar, to enrol recruits for service in General Sir Douglas Haig's British Expeditionary Force.

16.
The 28,000-ton German capital ship *Bayern*, which took part in the Baltic operations 1917. She was towed to Rosyth and broken up by Metal Industries Ltd, 1934-35. She was guided to her last berth by the three powerful Dutch tugs *Zivarte Zee, Witte Zee* and *Ganges*. Note the workmens' huts on the ship's hull.

17.
Flagship of the Commander-in-Chief of the German High Seas Fleet, 24,380-ton *Friedrich der Gross*, being broken for salvage in 1936-37.

18.
Air-locks being fitted to the W.W.I. German battlecruiser *Hindenburg* as a part of the raising in 1930. The tug *Sidonia* is to the right of the pontoon. Workmen are climbing the ladders to enter the locks. Of the Derfflinger Class, the 26,318-ton *Hindenburg* had taken part in action with the British light force fleet at Heligoland Bight, November 17th, 1917. She surrendered November 1918 and was scuttled here in Scapa Flow in June 1919. She was towed to Rosyth by the breakers Cox & Danks Ltd, 1931-32.

19. A detachment of the Lowland Mounted Brigade outside Letham Post Office and Storrar's Emporium, circa 1915. The brigade had made their Headquarters at Cupar.

20. Cpl. John Christie of the Highland Cycle Battalion at Leslie House Camp, July 1914. Under the orders of Black Watch officers the H.C.B. were part of Fife's coastal defence 1914-18.

21. Provost James Stark of Cupar greets Earl Haig at the unveiling of the Cupar War Memorial, 1925. Douglas Haig, 1st Earl Haig of Bemersyde was born in Edinburgh, June 19th, 1861, younger son of John Haig of Cameronbridge, West Fife. Haig was to have many Fife connections. He began his schooling at Paterson's School, Clifton Bank, St. Andrews, and was rector of St Andrews University, 1916-19, and its Chancellor 1922-28. The university mace was carried in his funeral cortege. With family connections in Fife, his nephew Lt. Col. Oliver Haig lived at Ramornie, Ladybank, Haig enjoyed his visits to Fife. He replaced Sir John French, 1st Earl of Ypres as Commander-in-Chief in France in 1915, and led the offensive against the Germans in 1918. Haig was a professional soldier of great distinction and indomitable resolution, but he had no strategic imagination and has been latterly blamed for his part in causing the carnage of W.W.I. For the last seven years of his life he expiated his part in Western Front action by working tenaciously for ex-servicemen, especially the maimed and blinded, as President of the British Legion. Haig died in 1928.

22. A view, under the Forth Railway Bridge, of the British Grand Fleet at Rosyth, after the Battle of Jutland, May 31st, 1916. Admiral John Rushworth Jellicoe's flagship H.M.S. *Iron Duke* is one of the vessels here.

23. Ratings and NCOs of the British Channel Fleet walk down to St. Andrews harbour, circa 1912. The Royal Navy regularly 'lay off' the East Neuk. Note the early Fife registration number SP4 on the car.

24. Women munitions workers at Messrs Barry, Ostlere & Shepherd, Kirkcaldy during 1914-18. Women took over mens' jobs in wartime, thus enhancing their chances of getting the vote more than all the militancy of the suffragettes.

25. Sybil Topham, Kate Bett, Cissie Keillor and Nessie Wilkinson pose while collecting money for the Red Cross (formed following the carnage of the Battle of Solferino, 1859) in Cupar, July 1918.

SOCIAL UNREST

WORKING-CLASS disappointment with Liberal Prime Minister Lloyd George's unfulfilled promises of a better standard of living following World War I, largely contributed to the country's social unrest. The miners were the main stormtroopers of the 'class struggle' and the General Strke of 1926 was the set piece of the conflict. The strike began on May 3 and lasted nine days, bringing the country to almost a standstill. Troops were used to ensure essential supplies and Dunfermline and Kirkcaldy became distribution centres for food and medicines. Troops guarded rail-heads and coal shipments. By May 12 only the coal miners continued to defy the Conservative Government of Stanley Baldwin.

Many workers in Fife saw the Russia of Josef Vissarionovich Stalin as the 'workers' paradise' they sought, and with the help of the Communist Party of Great Britain (founded in 1920) exploited local grievances towards 'revolution'. As the Russian revolutionary Grigori Eyseyevich Zinoviev noted when addressing the Congress of the Third International, July 1924: 'A Labour Government is the most alluring and popular formula for enlisting the masses in favour of a Communist dictatorship of the proletariat. We must make the most of the opportunities offered by such Labour Governments as, for instance, MacDonald's . . . The worker, peasant, railwayman will first do their revolutionary bit, and only afterwards realise that this actually is "the dictatorship of the proletariat".' Out of the political maelstrom in Fife came William Gallacher, elected in 1931 as MP for West Fife. He was Britain's first Communist MP and apologist for the horrors of Stalin's regime.

26.   A.J. Cook, secretary of the Miners' Union addresses a gathering of striking miners in West Fife. Cook was an inspired orator and described himself as 'a humble follower of Lenin'.

27. Fife Miners' Union leaders at the time of the 1920 Bowhill Strike. L to R: Willie Kirker; Dave Macmillan; Bert Cook; John Bird; Robert Houston.

28. Buckhaven workers' rally, 1921. As supporters of Lenin's philosophy their tableau lampoons the public image of Bolshevism as reported by the press.

29. Confrontation between rioter and police inspector. Photograph taken at the corner of Tolbooth Street, Kirkcaldy, at
8.15pm on the morning of June 13th, 1932. Organised by the National Unemployed Workers' Movement, Kirkcaldy
workers foregather to demonstrate against the Means Test of 1931. 933 workers had had their relief reduced and 244
others had been cut off from any benefit. Workers felt 'betrayed' that the National Government, led by Labour Prime
Minister Ramsay Macdonald, had 'cut their standard of living'.

30. Unemployed march from Kirkcaldy to Cupar, February 26, 1933. Here the procession has reached East March Street, Kirkcaldy. The Young Pioneers was a Communist Youth Movement for 9-14 year olds along the lines of the Russian 'All-Union Leninist Communist League of Youth', 1918.

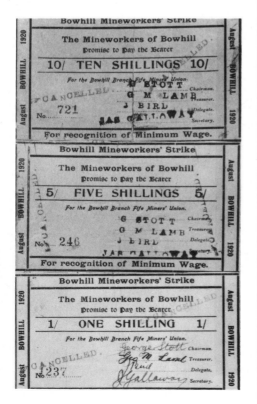

31. Strike pay tickets issued by the Bowhill Branch of the Fife Mineworkers Union, during the 1920 strike. They were called 'Birderies' after John Bird, one of the union officials. (See: Plate 27).

PEOPLE, PLACES, FACTS AND FACES

32. An impoverished, but characterful couple, pose outside Playfair Terrace and Ellice Place, St Andrews, in the early 1920s. The height of the gateposts has now been lowered and the gas lamp removed.

33.   A delightful picture of young and old outside a honeysuckle-covered cottage at Leuchars, circa 1910.

34.   The cobbled expanse of the High Street, Newburgh, looking East, circa 1924. J. Couttie & Sons making deliveries.

35. Pension day outside William Stocks's Post Office at Auchtermuchty. A pension of 5s. (25p) had been introduced by Prime Minister H.H. Asquith for all over 70 on January 1st, 1909.

36. Rosyth children celebrate the wedding of H.R.H. The Princess Elizabeth to 'Lieutenant Philip Mountbatten, RN' on November 20th, 1947.

37. Dunfermline's cobbled High Street, laced with tram rails, looking towards the Townhouse, circa 1922. The town had received a new set of municipal buildings 1876-79, designed by J.C. Walker of Edinburgh.

38. Rosyth's 1st Company of Boy Scouts with their leaders, 1914. Naval links are shown by the presence of a Sergeant Instructor.

39. The terrible winter of 1947 brought hardship and hazard to Fife. Here an East Neuk cottage struggles to maintain its identity against drifting snow.

40.   A tram on its way to Dunfermline clanks its way through Cowdenbeath High Street, circa 1914. By 1900 all the coal towns and industrial areas of W. Fife were linked by train and tram.

41.   Barefoot urchins chase Tram No 2 down the High Street, Leven. Arthur Gourlay's newsagent's and lending library was then a fare stage.

42. Banks were more competitive before World War I, and 'holding a presence' in town and villages was deemed important. The Clydesdale Bank's temporary premises shows a keeness to be represented.

43. The peace of Fife rural villages is seen here in this picture of Kilconquhar Main Street, before World War I. Note the open drainage for liquid household waste.

44. The Townhouse with its octagonal spire dominates the High Street, Strathmiglo, circa 1910.

45. Jock Anderson and his horse were a common sight in Dunfermline and Rosyth areas. John Scott of the High Street, Dunfermline, was one of the first butchers to expand deliveries.

46. A group of Inverkeithing children pose with their teacher in 1920 in front of their iron-fronted school. Corrugated iron proliferated as a building material after World War I.

47. North Street, St Andrews before the Younger Hall was built in 1929. In the distance the roadmen relay the road surface near St Salvator's chapel and Martyrs Church (1844).

48. Long dead movie stars and long forgotten white port enjoy publicity on this gable-end of a back street in Kirkcaldy. The advert of the Opera House tells us the year is 1930.

49. As the clock on St. Thomas's church, Newport-on-Tay, marks noon, Mr. Doig's wagonette waits at the foot of Cupar Road, circa 1912.

50. The barriers close on Station Brae, Newport-on-Tay, as a lone man waits for the coming train at East Newport station, around 1911.

FIFE FACES

51. A Strathmiglo village couple pose in their everyday clothes outside a weaver's cottage around 1910. Working-class clothes were of rough, thick material and were infrequently cleaned.

52. An East Wemyss cooper (ie, he made barrels) stands with his pipe-smoking wife at the door of their lodging, circa 1910.

53. A strathmiglo worthy fills her pail at the communal pump, circa 1914. Most of the landward villages of Fife had no piped water; some houses still had their old draw wells up to the late 1920s, when the Public Health Authorities compelled certain householders to erect water closets and do away with the stinking dry closets.

UNIVERSITY OF ST ANDREWS

THE university was founded 1410-13 and received its first charter from Henry Wardlaw, Bishop of St Andrews. This charter was confirmed and expanded by a series of Papal Bulls of Pope Benedict XIII, so that the university was a formal entity by 1414. St Andrews was the earliest university in Scotland.

During the period covered by this book the university had three Principals. Sir James Donaldson, during 1886-1915, became the first holder of the title of Principal of the University; his place was taken by Sir John Herkless who died in 1920. Sir James Irvine, then Professor of Chemistry took over, he also died in office in 1952. Irvine presided over many years of change and the foundation of new departments.

Among the photographs in this section are some which refer to the Students' Charities and the famous Kate Kennedy Procession. It would appear that the Kate Kennedy celebration originated in 1849 as an end of term 'rag' of the final year Arts students. On this occasion one of the students dressed up as 'Kate Kennedy', a niece of the famous bishop, and capered in the quad to the delight of his fellows. The ancient bell, called Katherine in the College Tower had long been called 'Kate Kennedy' although the girl herself is a shadowy figure in history. This 'rag' found instant popularity and became a symbol of undergraduate freedom. By the 1860s the 'rag' had spilled out into the streets of St Andrews, causing unpleasantness with the burghers. It was suppressed in 1882, but was revived in 1926 in the form of a historical pageant.

54.   Installation of Sir James Barrie as Rector, May 3rd, 1922. L to R: Dr James Younger of Mount Melville, the Chancellor's Assessor; Sir James Irvine, Principal and Vice-Chancellor (1921-52); Sir James Matthew Barrie, and, Field-Marshal the Earl Haig of Bemersyde, Rector, 1916-19.

55. Female students outside the old Union, North Street, St Andrews, with Jan Christian Smuts, the Premier of South Africa. Smuts, who fought in the Boer War on the Boer side was Rector of the University, 1931-34.

56. Student collectors of 'Charities' take time off in February 1938 to scale the old pump in the shadow of the striking spire of the parish church of Kingsbarns.

57. Principal Sir James Irvine with Stanley Baldwin, Chancellor of the University, 1929-47. Baldwin was Prime Minister from May 1923 to Jan 1924, and from Nov 1924 to June 1929; he served as Prime Minister in the National Cabinet of 1935-37.

58. The Kate Kennedy Procession of 1938. Kate, played by a male student, prepares to get into her coach with her 'uncle' James Kennedy, Bishop of St Andrews. Kennedy was the founder of St Salvator's College, 1450.

59. Charities procession, 1950. The floats make their way down South St, St Andrews, led by 'Pirates' out to 'rob' the public for the charity funds.

60. The Madrigal Singers dance an eightsome reel down at the harbour of St Andrews on the morning of May 1st, 1950. May morning has long been a day of celebration among St Andrews students marking the pre-Reformation devotion to the spirit of the May.

61. Graduation ceremony, 1934. Principal Irvine presides. That year the Italian inventor and electrical engineer, who developed the use of radio waves, Marchese Gugliemo Marconi, was Rector.

SONS OF THE SOIL

BY the early days of George V's reign, Fife farmers had embraced the new techniques of mechanisation available and the electrification of the countryside was achieved. Fife still had a great advantage in that its farmers were forward looking and the land did not suffer from absentee landlords. The landowners were still resident, were keen to develop crop rotation, expanded dairy farming, and introduced sugar beet amongst their rotations.

Numbers engaged in farming did drop considerably (by 20 percent of the workforce between 1881 and 1931), but the best land in Fife—particularly that of the East Neuk—was not wholly swallowed up by industrial growth. Permanent pastureland was reduced to 25 percent of the total area by 1939 (again reduced by 1950 to 16 percent), but Dr Johnson's reproach on Fife being almost treeless (in his famous exchange with Col John Nairne of St Andrews) was put right by the activities in the county of the Forestry Commission.

Fife farmers did suffer from the shrinking of the international markets following World War I, and began to have to shoulder enormous debts. World War II brought a further phase of prosperity. This enabled Fife to retain its reputation as one of the most important agricultural counties in Scotland with its rich soil and good husbandry. Fife still remained during 1910-50 one of the chief producers in Scotland of oats, wheat and barley. Potatoes became a profuse crop too, for the county, while turnips and swedes were also common.

62.   Ploughing matches were popular throughout Fife. Here in the East Neuk a team of fine horses are being made ready to plough a measured furrow in 1938. By 1909 the modern type of Clydesdale had been fixed.

63. The Fourth Prize Winner in the St Andrews and District Horse Parade 1932, shows itself off outside Henry Haggart's Newsagents, 63 Market Street. Note the ornate harness and the flower decorations.

64. Judges inspecting a ploughing match in East Fife in 1937. Fife horsemen were very proud of their charges. They organised their teams with military precision and discipline, taking great care with harness and brasswork.

65. Women 'singling' in the shadow of Wemyss Castle. Before the days of weed sprays, hand-hoeing was the chief method of keeping the land clean.

66. A trio of sheep from Sir John Gilmour's Montrave Estate spruced up for market in London. Time was when the difference in price between washed and unwashed wool made sheep-washing economic.

67. Horse-drawn binder harvests a field at Kenlygreen Farm, Boarhills, circa 1937. The foundation stone for Boarhills church was laid on Friday afternoon, March 23rd, 1866 by Provost Milton of St Andrews. The Churchyard contains the graves of those who perished in many a wreck along the East Neuk coast, notably the Swedish brig *Napoleon* of 1864.

68. Hand-sowing of grass-seed on wheat stubble to provide a follow-up hay product. Wemyss area, circa 1910. In those days artificial manure was also scattered by hand.

ST LEONARDS SCHOOL

THE school first opened its doors on October 2nd, 1877, and was set up in two houses at the bottom of Queen Street (now Queen's Gardens), St Andrews. Under the headship of Miss Louisa Lumsden (a pioneer in education, Miss Lumsden, later Dame Louisa, was Head Mistress from 1877 to 1881) the school was first known as St Andrews School for Girls and enrolled forty-four pupils, ten of them house girls. The opening of the school was one answer to the great need for 'a high class ladies' school' in the town and the promotion of education for girls, which was perfunctory in Scotland before 1870. The 'brainchild' of Mrs Matthew Rodger (wife of the minister of St Leonards Parish Church) and Mrs Lewis Campbell (wife of the Professor of Greek at the University), of the Ladies' Educational Association, the school had its own gymnasium and playground—an unheard of facility in girls' schools of the day, and looked upon with some trepidation by local residents! Physical drill, of course, was not a part of the Scottish Day School Code until 1895. At first the girls' work was examined by leading academics, but after 1887 pupils were entered for public examinations.

In 1883 the school changed its name to St Leonards, and was re-sited in its present location—on the site of the St Leonards college for 'poor clerks' founded in 1512. During the period covered by this book the school expanded; a Preparatory school was set up in 1894 in the fine Georgian house in North Street (now the Department of Fine Arts of the University) and named St Katherines.

69. A science class works in the school science building which was opened in 1908 by Sir Ernest Shackleton, who made four Antarctic Expeditions. Science was made prominent in the school curriculum when Miss Mary Bentinck Smith was Head Mistress (1907-21); by 1920 St Leonards was recognised as a teaching school for medical degrees at the University of London.

70. Visit to St Leonards on Saturday, October 1st, 1927, by H.R.H. The Duchess of York. This was the year of the school's Jubilee and the duchess opened the new library in Queen Mary's House. The duchess walks with Miss Katharine McCutcheon, Head Mistress 1922-38; behind walks the Rt. Rev C.E. Plumb, Bishop of St Andrews, Dunkeld and Dunblane, Chairman of Council, 1924-30.

FISHERFOLK AND FISHERWAYS

71. Her face lined with care, her dark clothes designed for hard work, this Anstruther fishwife chats with her neighbour as they wait for the milkman to call. Circa 1914.

72. Handing out biscuits on Anstruther quay. Prior to the departure of the winter herring fleet, fishermen handed out biscuits as good luck tokens for the coming voyage.

73. Fisherfolk gather to look at the catch on the quay at Largo harbour, circa 1910. The railway viaduct, over which trains first ran in 1856, stands in the background.

74. A Buckhaven fisherman 'redding' his lines, circa 1910. From this fishing term comes the dialect 'to redd', that is to sort out. It was thought very bad luck to have extraneous knots in the nets.

75. Boys running in the Wemyss Regatta Sports. These sports were held until 1939. Many of the East Neuk fishing villages had their annual fairs and sports, alas they have all died out.

76. At the age of 70, H.M. King George V died on January 20th, 1936. With traditional pomp and ceremony his son was proclaimed in East Fife burghs on January 25th, as Edward VIII. Here Baillie W. Fleming declares Anstruther's loyalty at the Cross.

77. I. Stevenson and T. Ritchie take their pallets to their boat. Pallets are the canvas and tar fishnet markers pioneered in Anstruther. In the background a Leyland Lynx DZ3 waits to be loaded with fish products.

78. Anstruther woman baiting the lines. Usually this was womens' work done by the relatives of fishermen. Bachelors often had to pay for someone to bait their lines if they had no time to do it themselves.

GOLF MEMORIES

CONTRARY to popular belief, golf was not 'invented' in Scotland, but owes its origins to the Romans who played a similar game during their *saturnalia*. Undoubtedly golf was played in Scotland from the early 15th century and by the 18th century St Andrews was dubbed the 'Alma Mater of the Golf'. Up to 1912 golf was free of charge to allcomers on the four courses at St Andrews; but, in that year a fee to visitors was instituted. The courses remained free to ratepayers until 1946.

If golf has a 'mecca' then it must be the Royal and Ancient Golf Club at St Andrews, whose present Clubhouse was opened in 1854. Before that the Club members—who had become the 'Society of St Andrews Golfers' on May 14th, 1754—met in the Union Parlour on the site of the modern students' residence of Hamilton Hall. The residence itself was established in 1949 in the old Grand Hotel once patronised by the famous and royal golfers who played the 'Old Course'. Incidentally, the Royal and Ancient Golf Club was given its 'Royal' title in January 1834 when King William IV agreed to become patron (he never visited St Andrews!).

Known world-wide, the 'Old Course' was first surveyed in 1836, in the days when there were no tees and none of the modern facilities around the Bruce Embankment. The 'Old Course' has changed little since 1913, but in 1953 management of the 'Old Course' was transferred from the Royal and Ancient Golf Club to the Joint Links Committee.

79.   Robert Tyre 'Bobby' Jones (1902-71), three times Open Golf Champion, crosses the last green of the 'Old Course' pursued by eager autograph hunters, 1936. Jones was made a Freeman of St Andrews in 1958.

80.   H.R.H. Prince George, Duke of York outside the Royal and Ancient Clubhouse. He took up captaincy of the R & A on Wednesday, Sept 24th 1930. Beside him stands the characterful Andrew Kirkcaldy the Club professional, 1910-33.

81. General Dwight David Eisenhower (1890-1969) walks across the first tee of the 'Old Course' with Roger Weatherhead and Col. Inglis, 1946.

82. American singer and actor Harry 'Bing' Crosby (1904-80) plays a practice shot, 1950. Most players play some practice shots before attempting the 'Old Course', noted by Bobby Jones in 1921 as 'the worst course on earth'.

WHO WAS THE BIGGEST COMEDIAN?

83. Scots comedian Harry Gordon, 'Laird of Inversnecky', a famous pantomime Dame, discusses a new script with Will
Fyffe—famous for his song, 'I Belong to Glasgow'—in the Christina Suite of Rusack's Marine Hotel, St Andrews. Plans
for Rusack's Marine Hotel (see plate 79 for its facade over the 'Old Course') were laid in 1885 and the hotel was open
for business in 1887. Founded by Wilhelm Rusack (a German who once had 'Rusack's Private Hotel', Abbotsford
Crescent), the hotel was one of the most famous in Scotland, and royalty stayed here many times. After World War II
the hotel was acquired by the Aberdeen Hotel Co Ltd, whose chairman was Will Fyffe (his daughter ran the 'hair salon'
within the hotel). In early December 1947, Fyffe had an operation on his inner-ear which resulted in dizzy spells. On the
morning of Saturday, December 6th, 1947, a number of golfers saw Fyffe topple and fall from the window of the
Christina Suite, Fyffe did not die instantly. He was rushed to St Andrews Cottage Hospital and died there at 4.30pm on
Sunday, December 7th. Many still believe that the Dundee-born comedian committed suicide.

84.   On March 12th, 1934, Sir Harry Lauder, appeared for a week at the Opera House, Dunfermline. Sir Harry visited several of the factories in Dunfermline with Provost McKay. He is seen here with staff of the Dunfermline Silk Mills. Harry Lauder (really Hugh MacLennan, 1870-1950) was one of the most famous stars of the music hall stage. Appearing in revue, he invariably wore a kilt and glengarry and carried a crooked stick. He was knighted in 1919 for his indefatigable entertaining of the troops on the French front during World War I.

85.   The funeral cortege of Admiral of the Fleet Rosslyn Erskine Wemyss, 1st Baron Wester Wemyss of Wemyss, June 1st 1933. A Member of the War Cabinet, 1918 Admiral Wemyss had died at his home at Villa Monbrillant, Cannes, and his body was transported to England by *H.M.S. Tempest*. His funeral oration at the Wemyss burial vault was given by Rev. J. Kennedy.

86. Baron Robert Baden-Powell (1857-1941), Chief Scout of the Boy Scout Movement he founded—the first camp was on Brownsea Island, Poole, Dorset, 1907—inspects E. Fife Scout Leaders between the wars.

87. Corporal John Ripley, VC—awarded in 1915 for conspicuous bravery at Rue de Bois, Battle of Aubers Ridge, Neuve Chapelle, France—talks to some likely recruits at the West Port, St Andrews. At the outbreak of World War I, Ripley had been retired from the army as a Colour Sergeant for two years and was a self-employed slater and chimney sweep. In 1914 he enlisted again in the 1st Battalion Black Watch and acted as a Recruiting Sergeant in East Fife. Although he belonged to Montrose, Ripley lived most of his life in St Andrews; He was the only St Andrews man to win a VC. He was one of the oldest VC winners and the only holder of the Long Service Medal to gain the highest bravery award. When he returned to St Andrews after being decorated by the King, he was given a tremendous reception. Ironically, he died from injuries sustained by falling off a ladder at Castlecliffe in 1933 in the course of his duties as a window cleaner.

VEHICLES GREAT AND SMALL

88. D. Barrie's 4-ton Dennis (the model had been withdrawn in 1933) coal lorry comes to grief at Anstruther harbour.

89.   Elie station before its reconstruction of 1920. The station had been built in 1863, and added to in 1900.

90.   A member of the St Andrews Motor Club's MG gets stuck in the mud and has to rely on horseflesh to pull free.

91.   T. Lister of Crossgates classic shot of a tram in Halbeath Road, Dunfermline, stuck in a snowdrift, March 17th, 1914.

92. Frank West of Cardenden and his horse 'Miss'; he charged miners 3/6 (17½p) for a 'flitting'—not always 'min-licht!'

93. Tar being transported by barrel from Kirkcaldy Gas Works to the railway station to be taken to Grangemouth. The cart is passing Bennochy Bridge, Kirkcaldy, circa 1936.

94. Robert McCarroll steam roller, No 13, works along Dysart Road, by Ravenscraig Park wall, Kirkcaldy. Work was being done on the Kirkcaldy to Dysart tramway, opened January 20th, 1911.

95. The Burgh of Buckhaven, Methil and Innerleven's steam driven 'Merryweather' fire engine, circa 1910. By World War I, Merryweather were changing their fire engines to combustion driven.

96. After the first motor show in 1896, at the Imperial Institute, motor cycles became very popular. This model of circa 1910 is proudly being shown off by its owner—he would reverse his cap and wear goggles while speeding along. In 1925 motor cycling became a craze for women.

97. Not a 'space vehicle' from popular author H.G. Well's (1866-1946) *War of the Worlds*, but a motorised mine rescue team from Leven, pre-1914.

98. Clackmannan Coal Owners Rescue Teams visit West Fife mining areas to give first aid demonstrations, circa 1920.

99   The fleet of battery electric 1-ton vans (3½hp, 19mph) belonging to Messrs Barry, Ostlere & Shepheard Ltd, at the now demolished Walton Inlaid Linoleum works, Kirkcaldy. Linoleum had been invented by Frederick Walton in 1860.

100.   Fire Tender No 3 and power unit of Dunfermline City Fire Brigade, circa 1930. Bedford 6-cylinder vans were often used as 'back-up' vehicles for regular fire engines.

101. Char-á-banc driver and passengers pose, circa 1924. This was the Fettykill Office Drive round Glenfarg of the 1920s.

102. Conductresses 22 and 20 stand in celluloid immortality with bus K22 of the General Motor Coaches Co. Ltd, circa 1922. G.M.C.C Ltd, operated out of Kirkcaldy.

103. Nicknamed 'the gondola of the working classes' the trams complemented the railway service in West Fife. Britain's first passenger tramway was opened at Birkenhead in 1860. Trams sparked their way through Lochgelly every 6 minutes. Dunfermline and District Tramways Co operated from November 2nd, 1909 to July 5th, 1937.

104. The open-topped trams of Kirkcaldy Corporation were popular for sunny afternoon jaunts. Tram No 13, bound for Whyte's Causeway, passes the then new library building, Kirkcaldy. The peak year for trams was 1919-20. Glasgow was the last big city to have a regular tram service, continuing until 1962. The top of a tram was a favourite place with Fifers for courting. Kirkcaldy Tramways, in their dark olive green and cream livery, operated February 28th, 1903 to May 15th, 1931. One other Fife tramway company operated too, that of Wemyss & District Tramway Co, from August 25th 1906 to January 31st, 1932.

105. Kincardine Bridge swings open to allow a ship to pass. Build in 1936, the bridge is a little more than half a mile long and has a span of 100 yards.

106. The Glen Bridge, Dunfermline, opened April 20th, 1932, by Provost T. Gorrie, and cost £40,379.

107. One of the SES's fleet of Morris Z vans (the model was introduced in 1940) outside a floodlit Holy Trinity Church, St Andrews, 1950. Electricity had replaced gas as street lighting in Fife by the late 1930s. Despite the nationalisation of the electricity boards in 1949, places like Gauldry and Balmerino did not receive electricity until the early 1950s.

108. William Wilson, his sons and staff, stand in Wilson's South St garage, St Andrews, 1908. A blacksmith by trade, Wilson realised that the combustion engine was 'the coming thing', so he changed his horses for cars.

109. A Maudsley Landelect (1910), driven by Ernest Philp, conveys Ex-Provost Wilson, Provost Boase and Town Clerk Cargill Cantley in the 1935 Jubilee parade. The car—note the phoney number plate—has reached the junction of North Street and Union Street, St Andrews. The car carries an Automobile Association (founded 1908) badge.

110. A 'big hoose' open-top tourer—with glum chauffeur—at Falkland, circa 1910. Many of the 'gentry' bought foreign cars which had once belonged to Europe's aristocracy.

111.   Scottish Motor Cycle speed racing, St Andrews, 1950—probably the last time it was held after starting in 1908.

112.   St Andrews Merchants' Association trip from St Andrews station (est. 1850), circa 1914. Incidentally the Bank Holiday was sponsored by Sir John Lubbock (1834-1913), Liberal MP for Maidstone and Rector of St Andrews University, 1907-10.

113.   Air Display at Leuchars, September 1950, to celebrate the Battle of Britain, July–September 1940. Leuchars RAF
Station had been one of Britains leading airfields since World War I.

114.   A Harvard which made a forced landing at Strathtyrum gates, near St Andrews, August 1950.

ONE DAY THIS HAPPENED . . .

FROM cock-fighting and barrel organs to street fairs and Sunday school trips in hay carts, the accent on entertainment and social activities changed enormously in Fife during the period 1910 to 1950; the emphasis changing particularly from inexpensive fireside amusements to paid diversions.

World War I altered tastes and demands. Leisure entertainments during the harsh years of World War I, were largely geared to the low quality demanded by the soldiers on leave and the mass of working-class civilians, working harder and longer, but with more cash to spend. The cinema, for instance with its cheap seats gave them the easy entertainment they wanted. There was some public concern in Fife that morality would suffer from the escapism and sensationalism of the cinema freely attended by both sexes in the dark. Thus were usherettes 'trained to watch for offences' against public morality stirred on by the Kirk Sessions who saw the horrors of war as no excuse for 'lowering standards'. Indeed the war made boom years for the cinema, the concert and the home entertainment, for in 1915 professional football was abandoned and alcoholic sales were restricted.

The officers and the upper classes indulged in a craze for dancing and jazz. Complex dances like the fox-trot became popular, and old conventions like not dancing with same partner twice running were abandoned at social gatherings. What these photographs show is how functions must have been dull by modern standards and how rapidly public sophistication increased with the Armistice signed on November 11th, 1918.

115. Cockfighting—illegal since 1849—at Lochgelly, 1914. Jock Watson of Westfield and Sandy Blair of Gammy Place, bred fighting cocks.

116. Cardenden 'Dixie Dance Band', popular during 1914-18. Here banjo player Tom Armile leads the band in the 'smash hit' fox-trots.

117. Once one-man bands were legion in Fife streets, particularly during the Depression. A war vetern entertains East Wemyss children with his own idiosyncratic music.

118.   Lammas Fair, South Street, St Andrews, 1947. The oldest surviving medieval market in Scotland, it takes its name from the pre-Refomation feast of the 'first fruits', August 1st.

(Overleaf)
119.   Fronted by a contingent from the Royal Air Force, Leuchars, Sheriff J.C. Fenton, K.C., reads the Proclamation of H.M. King George VI, at Cupar Cross, on December 15th, 1936.

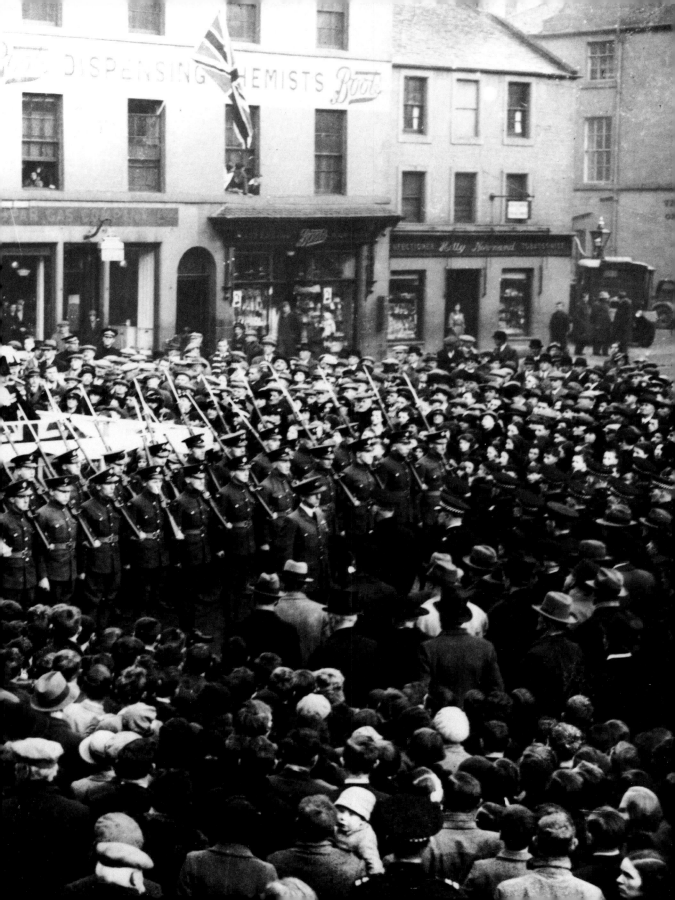

120. The Beach, Lundin Links, circa 1928. This part of Fife's coastline was developed from Victorian days as a holiday resort and golfing area.

121. Auld Bucket Pans, Kirkcaldy foreshore, circa 1900. Here salt was once gathered for use in the herring packing process.

122. 'The Batchelor Boys', a party of beach entertainers, St Andrews, circa 1914. Such 'Pierrot' shows were introduced from France in the 1890s.

123. Leslie Market and Fair, circa 1913, photograph taken of its original site on The Green. In the foreground is an early Fish and Chip vendor.

124.   A hospital fund-raising pageant, circa 1932, Dunfermline. In the days before the National Health Service hospitals relied on public funding for extra equipment.

125.   A flower day for charity at Cupar Cross, circa 1934. Note the lamps in the background removed in World War II for scrap.

126. A face that encouraged no complaints! An itinerant organ grinder and her monkey, entertain in Playfair Terrace, St Andrews. She toured the streets with her cacophonous music during the Lammas Market.

127. A Sunday School picnic outing, circa 1912. Compare the well-scrubbed children in the cart with the barefoot urchins in the Kirkcaldy street scene.

128. A group of Pathhead—near Kirkcaldy—parishioners prepare for an outing in 1910. An interesting study in pre-World War I attire for men, and in facial hair!

129. A crowded Step Rock Pool, St Andrews, July 1948. The sunbathing tiers were an innovation patronised throughout the year.

130. The Ancient Mercat set out in the High Street of the fishing centre of Pittenweem, August 1934. A group of 'big hoose' chauffeurs stand in the foreground.

131. SP 708 was the first car—belonging to the builder Mr Walker Horne—over the new Lower Largo Bridge.

132. Charity sports day held by the Lowland Mounted Brigade, August 1917. The L.M.B. and Lanarkshire & Yeomanry soldiers were patients at the Edenfield V.A.D. Hospital, Springfield, during World War I.

SOME ROYAL VISITS TO FIFE

KING George IV was the first reigning monarch to visit Scotland since Charles II had been crowned King at Scone on January 1st, 1651. George's niece Queen Victoria, crossed Fife, via North Queensferry, Inverkeithing and Cowdenbeath, on her way to Balmoral on Tuesday, September 6th, 1842. Yet, neither she, nor her son, Edward VII, ever paid an 'official royal visit' to Fife; but, on September 27th, 1876, Queen Victoria's fourth son, the haemophiliac Prince Leopold, Duke of Albany, played himself in as Captain of The Royal and Ancient Golf Club. On that occasion he was a guest of John and Lady Catherine Whyte-Melville at Mount Melville, near St Andrews.

The royal visits long remembered in Fife were those of H.M. King George V and Queen Mary during July-August 1923. They were accompanied by the popular Duke and Duchess of York and were hosted by the Earl and Countess of Elgin at Broomhall, near Dunfermline. Queen Mary made a separate visit to Falkland and Cupar as pictures in this section show. On her visit to East Fife, Queen Mary was accompanied by the Lord Lieutenant Sir Ralph Anstruther of Balcaskie. Queen Mary lunched at the House of Falkland, and via Freuchie, Ladybank, and Melville House, where she was entertained by Mrs R.S. Melville, she journeyed to Cupar where she laid a wreath at Cupar War Memorial.

133. Provost R. Osborn Pagan presents his wife to H.M. Queen Mary at the steps of Cupar War Memorial on Thursday, August 30th, 1923.

134. The Earl of Elgin and Kincardine, Lord Lieutenant of Fife, accompanies H.R.H. Edward, Prince of Wales, to honour the dead of World War I at Kirkcaldy. Behind stands Archie Provand of Dairsie, a prominent British Legion area representative.

135. H.M. Queen Mary is welcomed at the gates of Falkland Palace by Master Michael Stuart, Hereditary Custodian of the Palace. Behind stand Lt. Col. the Hon. Charles Maule Ramsay and Mrs Maule Ramsay. The young Custodian clutches his bonnet which had fallen at the Queen's feet as he bowed!

136.   King Peter of Yugoslavia, while inspecting the Polish Troops in Fife, visited St Andrews University. He walks through St Mary's Quad, between the Polish President in exile M. Wladyslaw Raczkiewicz and Principal Sir James C. Irvine, September 1942. King Peter, a naturalised British citizen, then 19, was forced into permanent exile by the Communist regime; he died in 1970 at Denver, Colorado, USA.

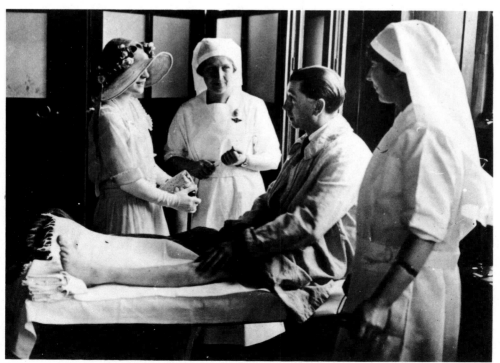

137.   H.R.H. The Duchess of York, visits Dunfermline Hospital, 1923. The Duke and Duchess of York were guests at Broomhall at the time.

138. 'Jings wull she speak tae me?' H.M. Queen Elizabeth talks to Brownies and Cub Scouts during her visit to Crail, 1950.

A SOCIETY WEDDING

139. The newly-weds Ismay Catherine, elder daughter of Lord Ninian Chrichton Stuart of Falkland, and John Anthony Hardinge Giffard, 3rd Earl of Halsbury and Viscount Tiverton, walk through the gateway of Falkland Palace after their wedding, Oct 1st, 1930.

140. The couple's wedding procession preparing to leave for the reception at the House of Falkland. The Palace front faces the High Street of Falkland burgh.

WORLD WAR II: 1939-1945

141. The Rt. Hon. Winston Leonard Spencer Churchill, Prime Minister and Minister of Defence, 1940-45, strides out along the West Sands, St Andrews, during a 'secret' visit with Chiefs of Staff. On his right his wife Clementine sports a military greatcoat against an icy wind, and wears a wartime 'turban hat' for which she became famous. On Churchill's left walks General Vadislav Sikorski, Prime Minister of the Polish Government in exile and Commander-in-Chief of the Polish forces. Sikorski was killed in an aircraft accident at Gibraltar, 1943.

142. Features set in a typical repose which earned him the name of 'The British Bulldog', Prime Minister Churchill stands at a secret rendevous near st Andrews with General Sikorski and General Paszkiewicz. In 1942 Paszkiewicz unveiled a panel set in the west wall of the Town Hall, Queens Gardens, St Andrews, showing the appreciation of the Polish soldiers for the local hospitality extended to them.

143. Their Majesties the King and Queen pose with General Sikorski while inspecting military installations near St Andrews, 1942.

144. Churchill, Sikorski and Paszkiewicz take the salute of an armoured convoy on the Dairsie-St Andrews road, 1942.

145. East Wemyss children try out their new gas masks in September, 1939. By January 1940 most people stopped carrying gas masks as gas attacks by the Germans were thought unlikely.

146. St Andrews women watch a demonstration of a gas-mask-cum-cot (Government Issue) for a baby, 1940.

147.   A wartime Royal Observer Corps team at a monitoring station in Dunfermline.

148.   Regular casualty practices took place during wartime. This one was enacted at Dunfermline. Note the special breathing apparatus.

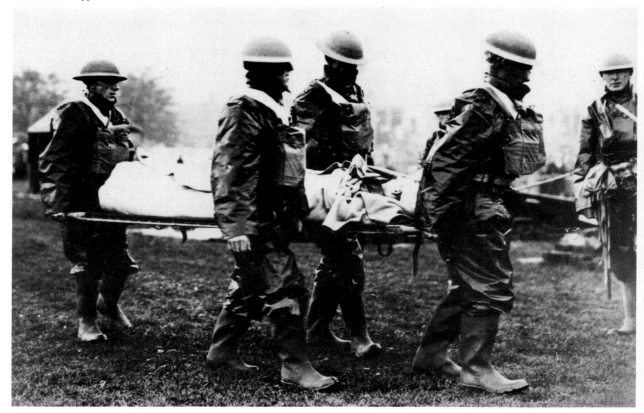

149. Casings for 6-ton bombs awaiting despatch to ordnance depots where the explosive charges would be fitted. Such casings were made at Nairn's, Kirkcaldy, during World War II.

150. The GPO's attempt to discourage customers? No, sandbagging preparations against air-raids at St Andrews Post Office, South Street, soon after the declaration of war with Germany, September 3rd, 1939.

151. Under the watchful eye of a pipe-smoking corporal, a bomb squad prepare to remove an unexploded bomb at Boarhills in the early years of the war.

WORK FOR ALL

152.   A workman loads a weighing machine at Dunfermline Gas Works. Clement Attlee's Labour Government nationalised
Fife's municipal and private gas companies, May 1st, 1949.

153. James Christie, Fire Master and his eight firemen, with Sandy Petie driving, pose at the West entrance to Mount Melville Lodge with the St Andrews fire engine, circa 1935.

154. Jimmy Carson, the St Monance Bellman, 1934. Carson was one of the last of the East Fife Town Criers.

155. The Merryweather Steam Engine belonging to the City of St Andrews takes part in a Fire Drill by the bridge over the Swilken Burn on the Old Course. The fire engine was presented to St Andrews in 1901 by Colonel Lindsay Carnegie. The engine was in use up to 1921.

156. Bowhill Pit Lassies, circa 1936. Women worked at the pithead sorting the stones from the coal. These redoutable young women were employed by the East Fife Coal Company. Ten men lost their lives in an explosion at this colliery on October 31st, 1931.

157. Workmen make safe subsidence at Wemyss Coal Company's colliery, circa 1935. The Wemyss family of Castle
      Wemyss (of historic interest for the first meeting between Mary, Queen of Scots, and Henry, Lord Darnley, her future
      husband, 1565) had been exporting coal and salt from Methil dock for hundreds of years when Randolph Gordon
      Erskine Wemyss succeeded to the family estates in 1864. The Wemyss coal field (covering the parishes of Dysart,
      Markinch, Scoonie and Wemyss, and under the Forth) had brought good pay packets to the area from the days of the
      Franco-Prussian War (1870-71) when French, German, Dutch and Danish ships crowded the East Neuk harbours. The
      Wemyss family invested money in expanding and updating the Methil docks, and by 1913 a new 40-acre dock was
      opened at Methil and by the beginning of World War I the dock was exporting over 2.5 million tons of coal to Europe.

158. Guardbridge Paper Mill from the air, note the now-defunct railway system, circa 1939. Once the port for St Andrews and Cupar, the 14th century bridge of Bishop Henry Wardlaw here carried the main artery to the East Neuk. In 1873 a distillery complex was bought by the Guardbridge Paper Co and was developed into a paper mill.

159. Steeplejacks atop the chimney of West Pinlaws Mill, Leslie. Maintenance was being carried out by Isaac Schoolbraid & Sons, circa 1936.

160. Logan Martin Church spire being repaired by Messrs Isaac Schoolbraid & Sons, Leslie. D.B. Schoolbraid defies gravity on a rickety ladder above the spire.

161. Girls working a pressing machine at Brown's Laundry, Dunfermline, circa 1940.

162. Interior of a weaving shed, Pleasance Linen Works, Falkland, circa 1936. Once Falkland was the centre of the handloom weaving industry.

ANDREW CARNEGIE

THE son of a damask-linen weaver, Andrew Carnegie was born at Dunfermline on November 15th, 1835. In 1848 his parents—'poor but honest . . . of good kith and kin'—emigrated to America, settling in Allegheny, Pennsylvania. Beginning work as a weaver's assistant in a cotton factory, Carnegie went on to be a telegraph operator. Ultimately as superintendent of the Pittsburgh division of the Pennsylvania Railroad Company, Carnegie laid the foundation of his fortune by the introduction of sleeping cars in the railway and by his successful investments in oil lands near Oil City. After the American Civil War, 1861-65,—in which Carnegie was in charge of the military railroads—Carnegie began his great work of developing the Pittsburg iron and steel industries. Carnegie's work became the basis for the US Steel Corporation. On his retirement he lived in baronial style at Skibo 'Castle' in Sutherland, and developed his philanthropic work. He spent £10,000,000 alone on the provision of libraries in the English-speaking world, and in 1903 founded the Dunfermline Trust with an income of £25,000 for the improvement of his native town. Carnegie died in 1919 at Lenox, Massachusetts, USA.

163. The Education (Scotland) Act of 1908 gave school boards permission to provide medical examinations for children. Legal action could now be taken against parents whose children were dirty or verminous. Dunfermline was the first Scottish burgh to provide such free medical treatment. The Carnegie Trust helped to provide a College of Hygiene and Physical Education at Dunfermline in 1905. Here children are being examined for head lice and treated for skin diseases at the Dunfermline Public Baths, 1926.

164. Andrew Carnegie was elected Lord Rector of St Andrews University in October 1901, and was re-elected in 1904 to serve until 1907. In June 1901 Carnegie established the Trust for Universities in Scotland and a huge endowment income was enjoyed by the universities of St Andrews, Aberdeen, Glasgow and Edinburgh. Part of the fund too, went to paying the fees of deserving students. Carnegie's wife also gave funds in 1904 for women's union facilities at St Andrews and Dundee.

165. Carnegie Gymnasium, Dunfermline, around 1929. Physical education was one of Carnegie's great interests and his gifts of equipment and premises were very much in the spirit of the Education (Scotland) Act of 1908.

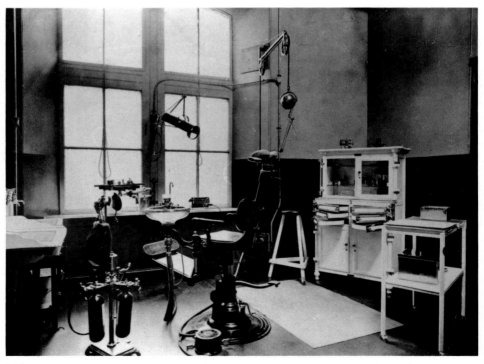

166. The Dental Clinic, Carnegie Baths, Dunfermline, circa 1930. Dunfermline was one of the first places in Scotland to give free dental treatment because of Carnegie's endowments.